This book is belongs to

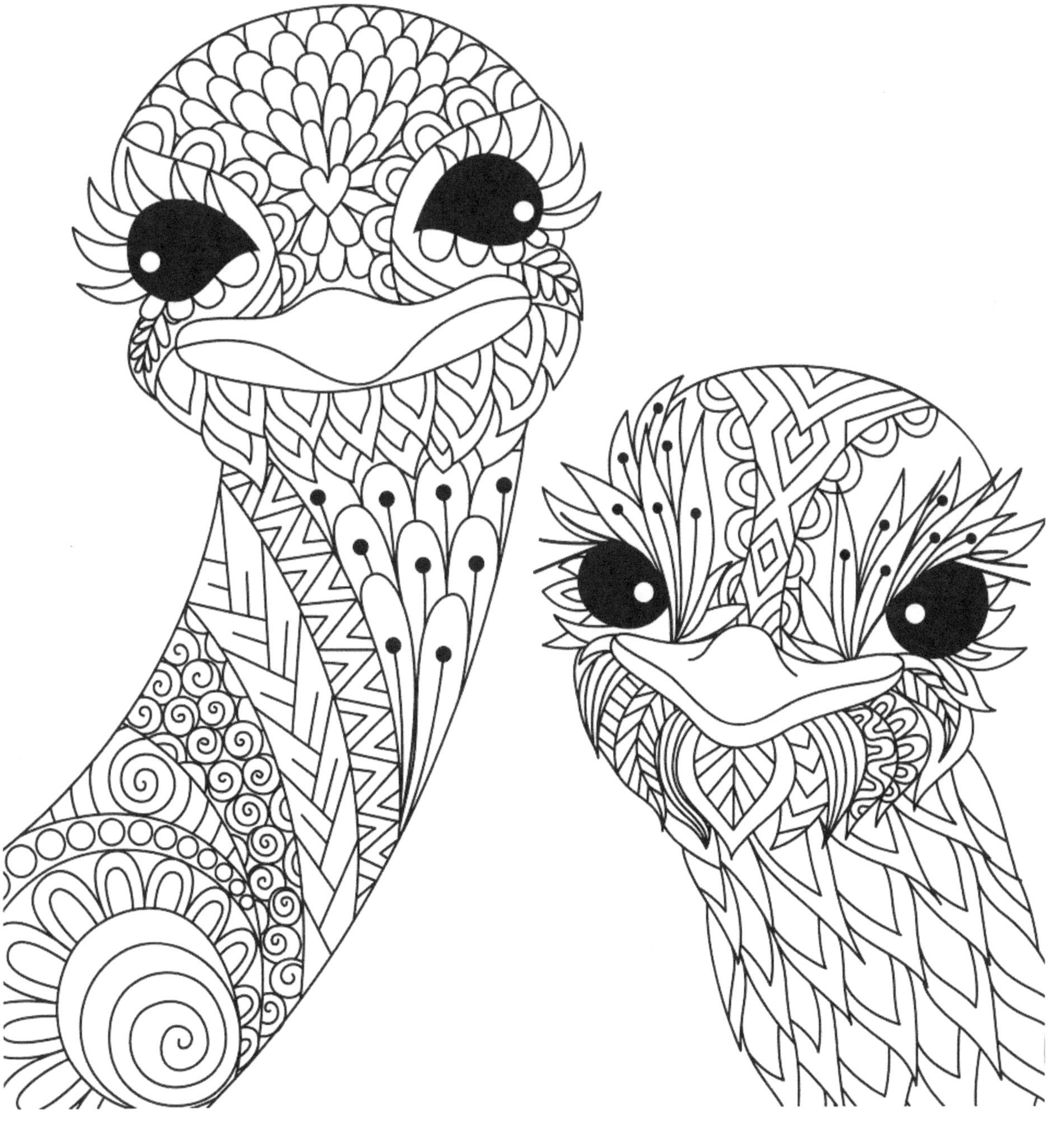

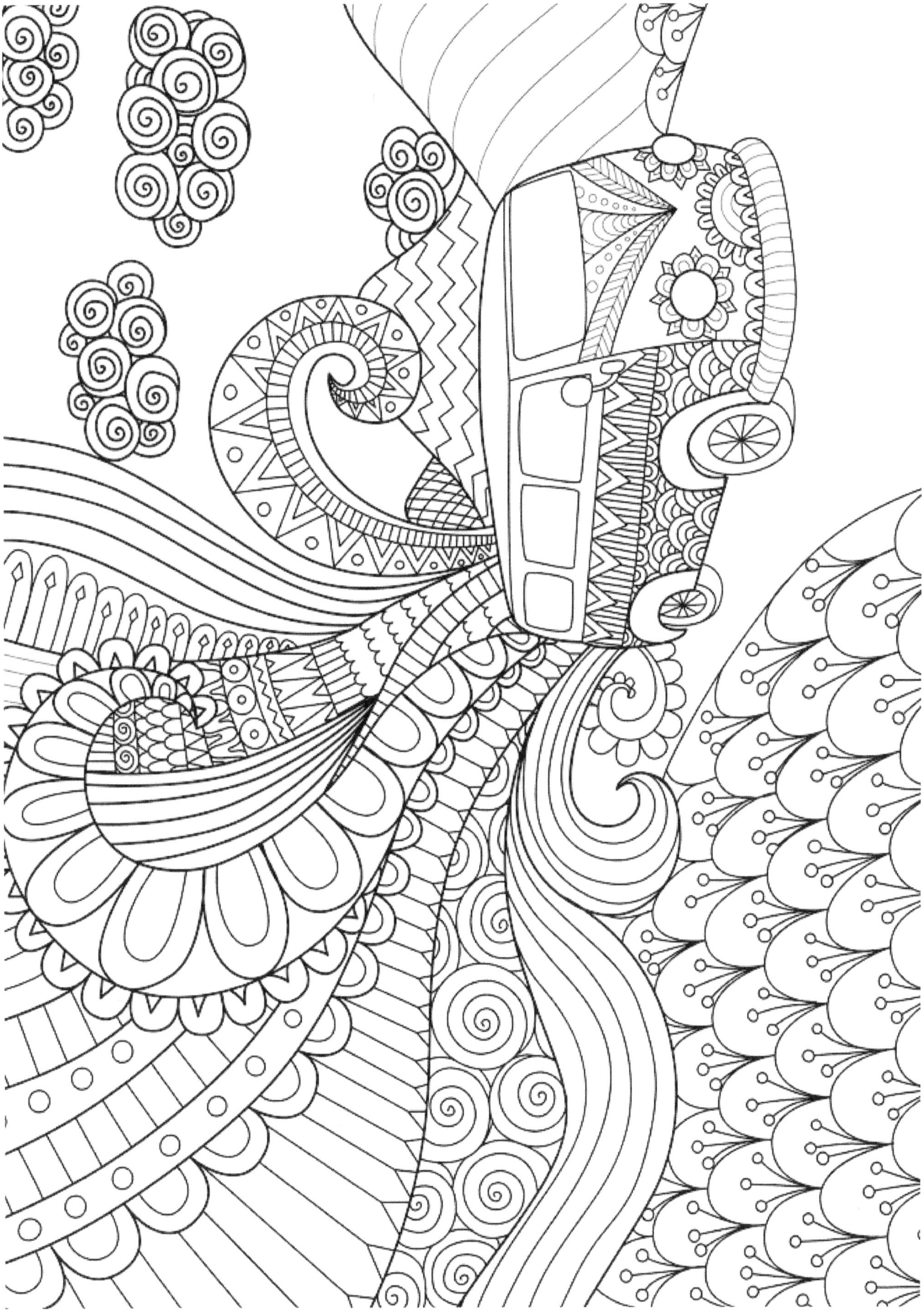

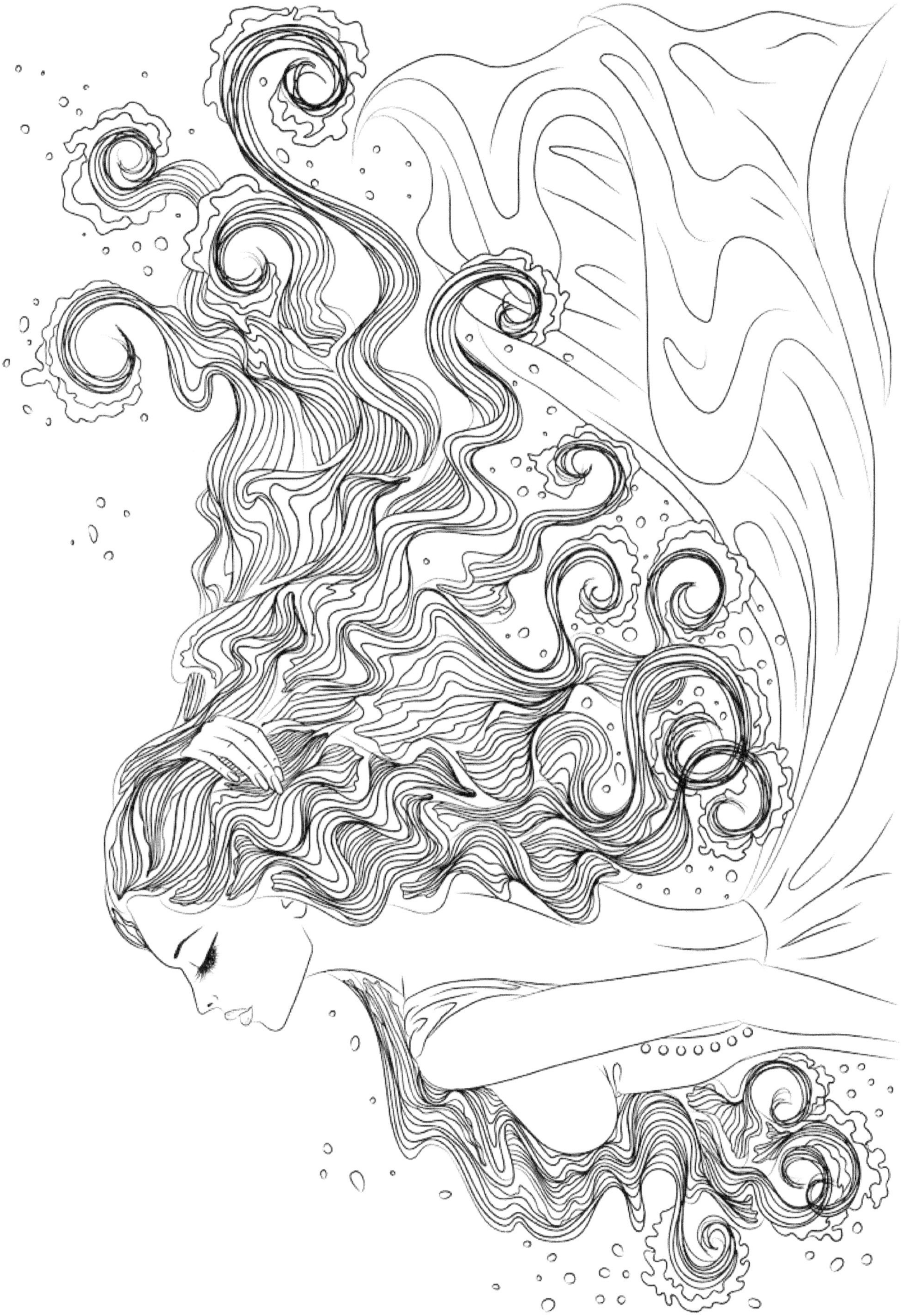

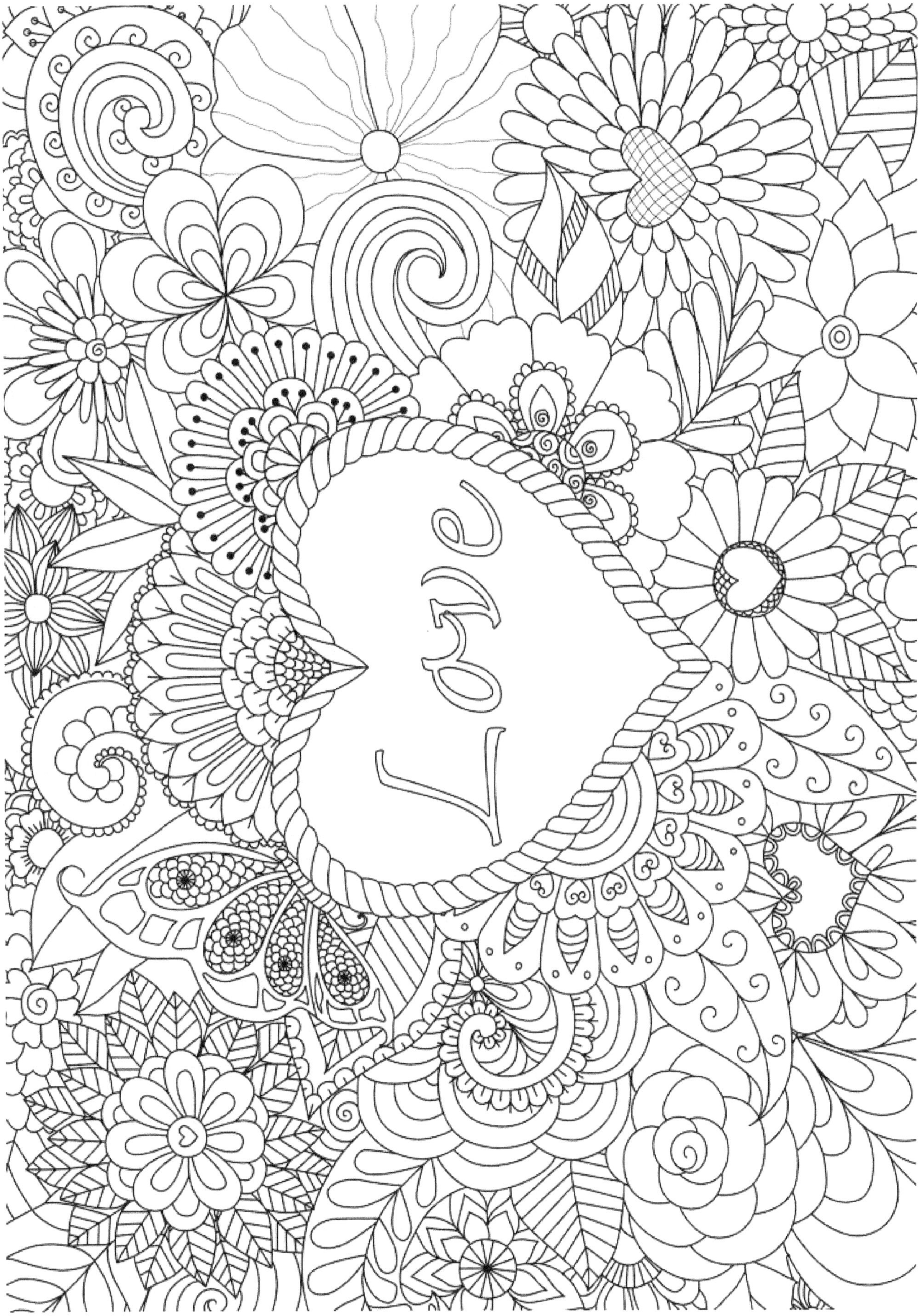
Love

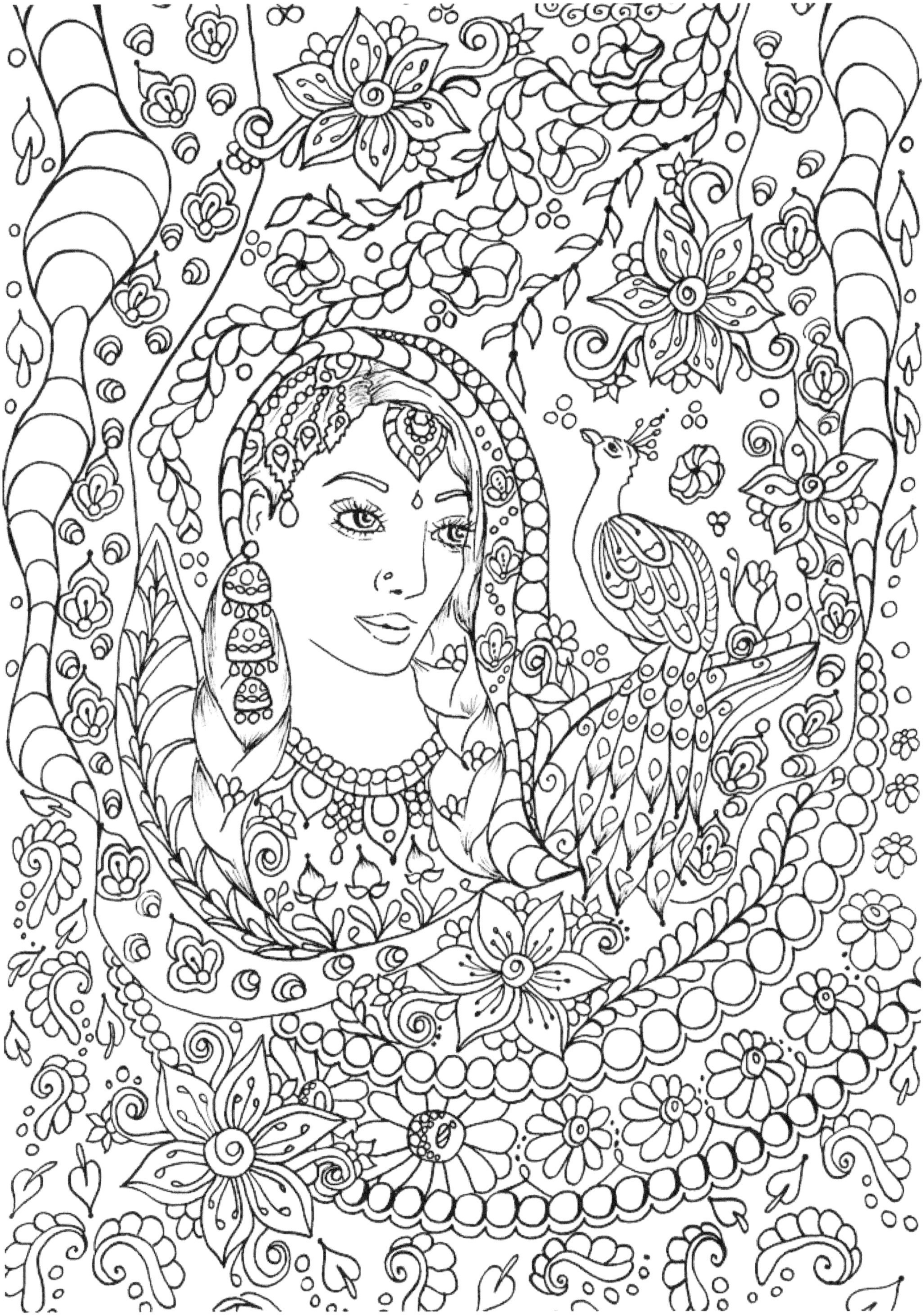

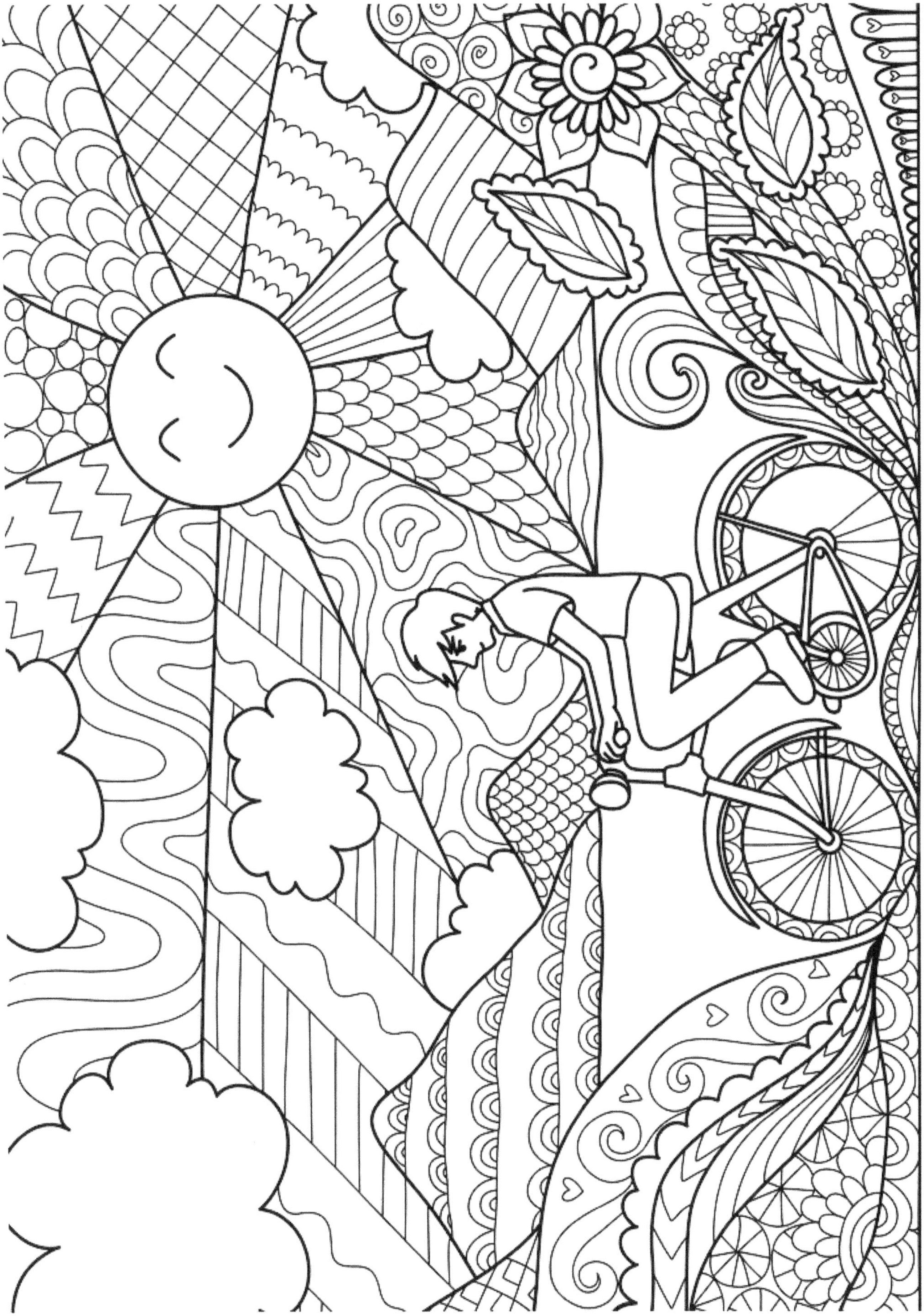

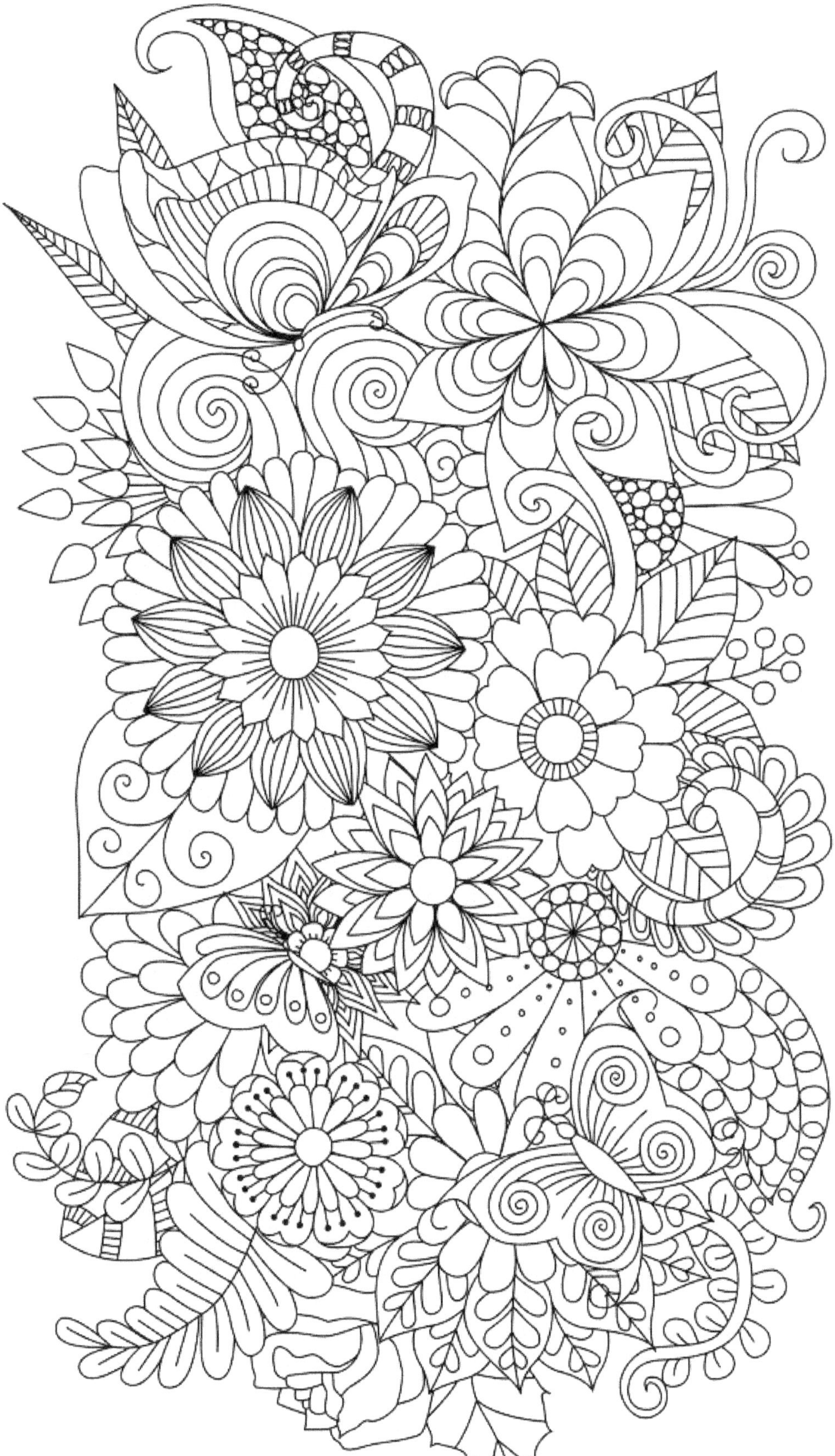

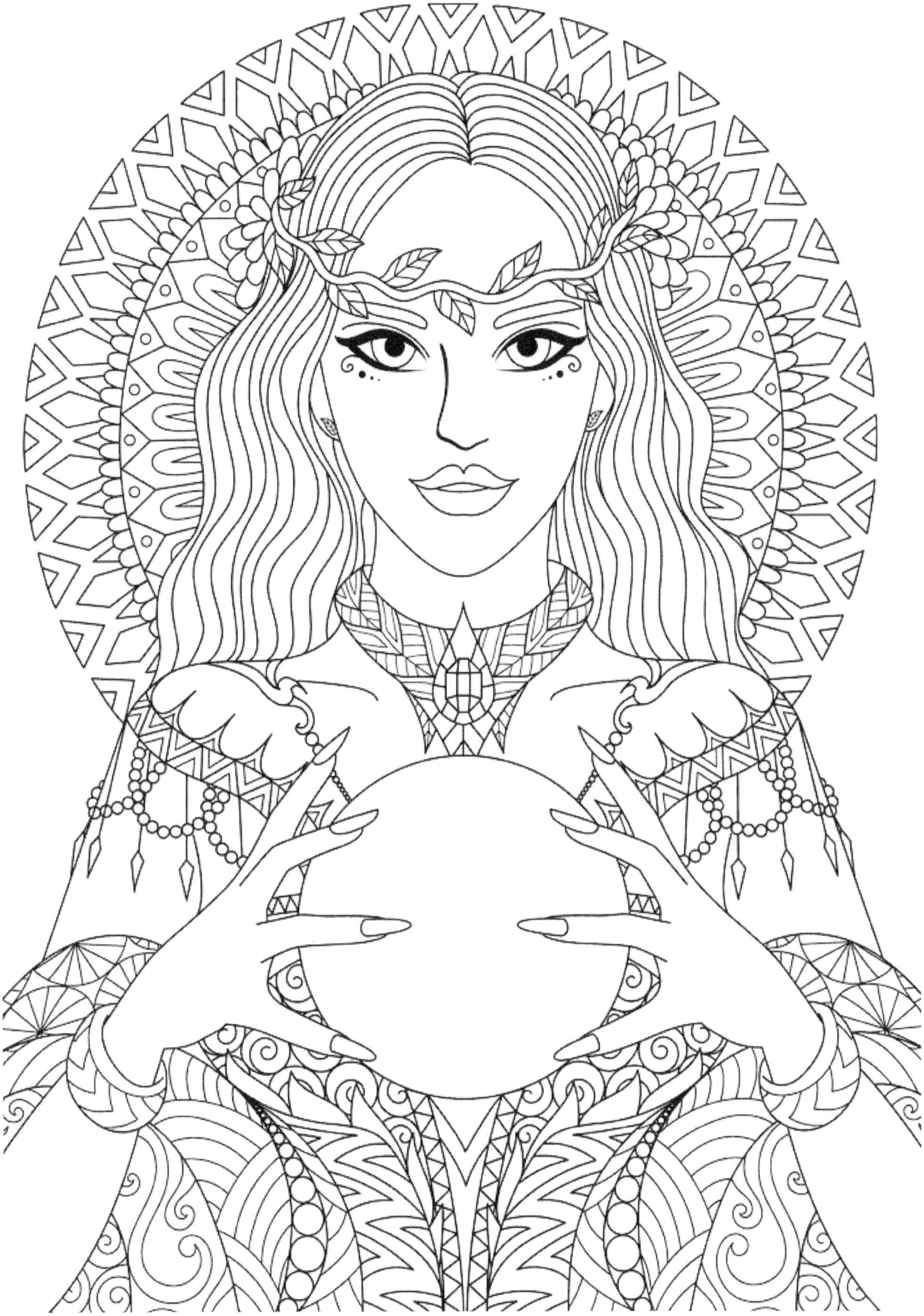

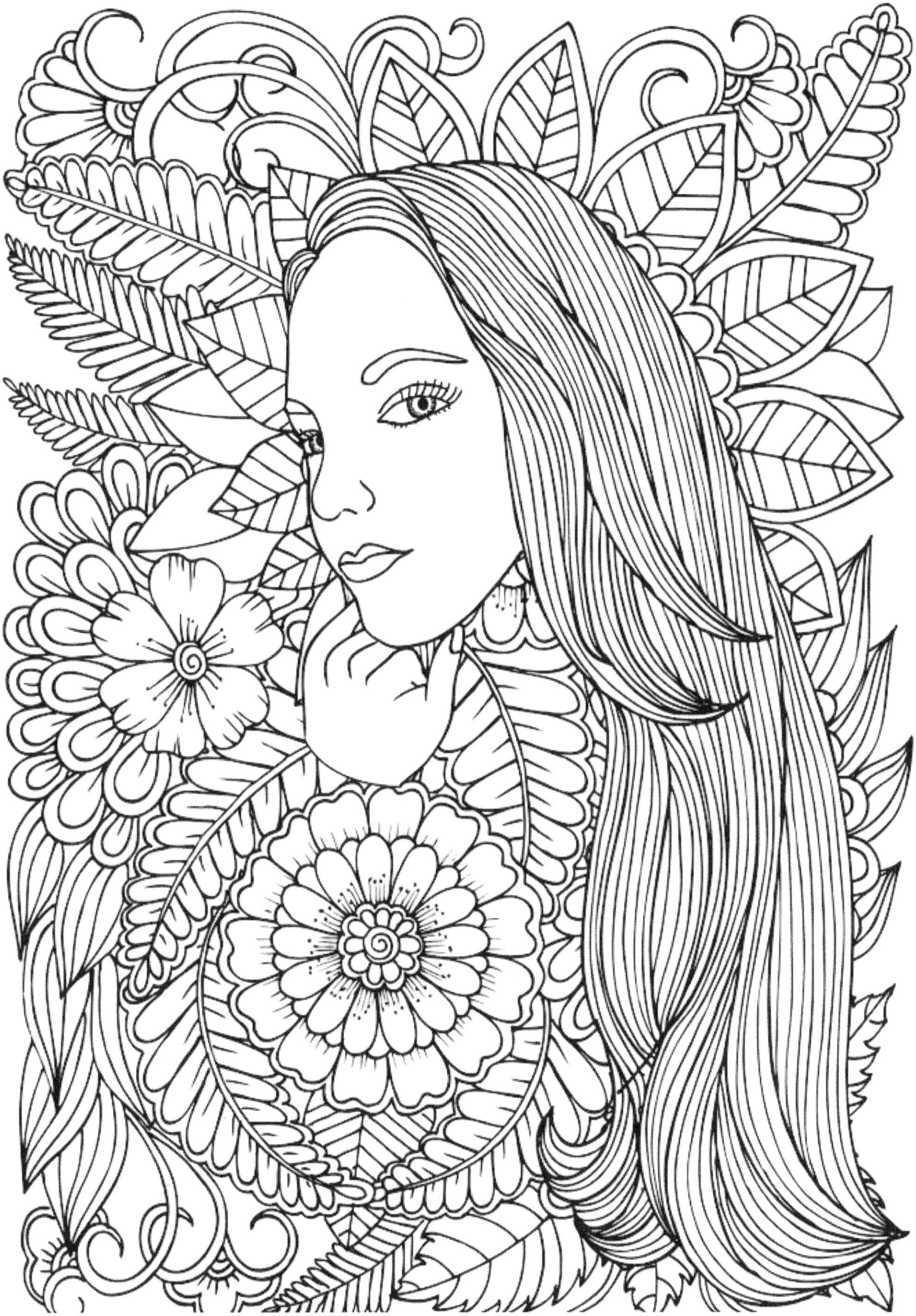

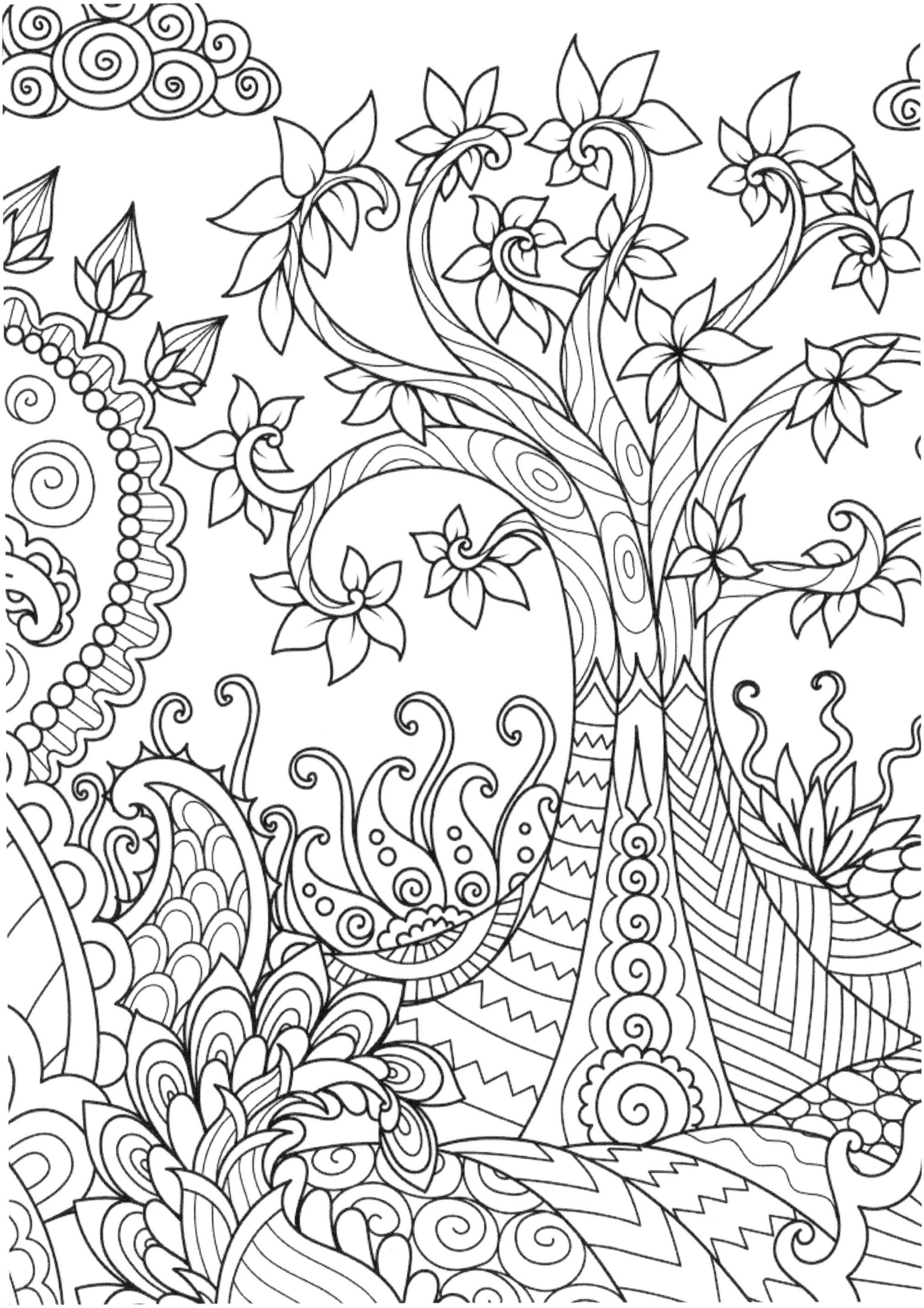

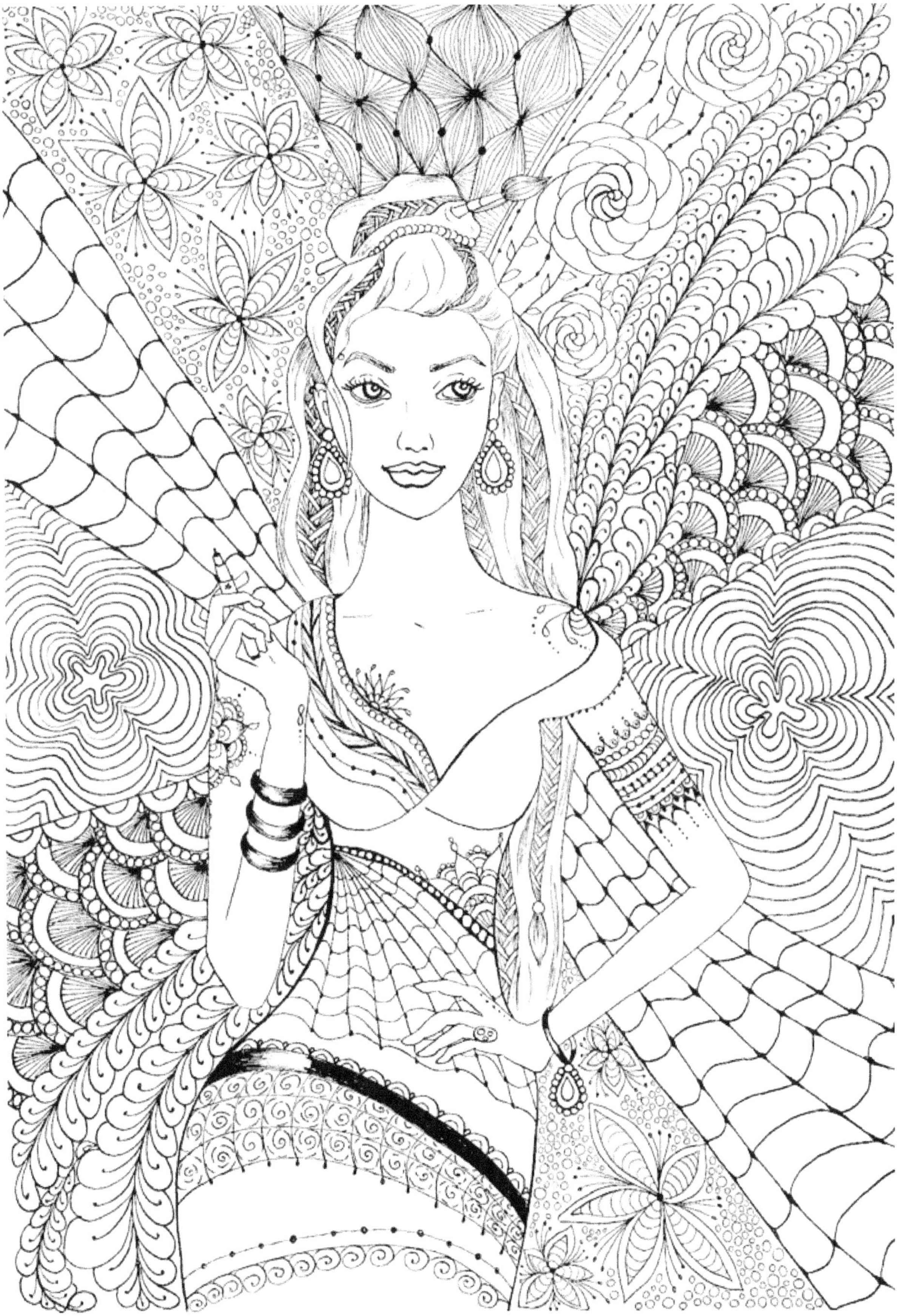

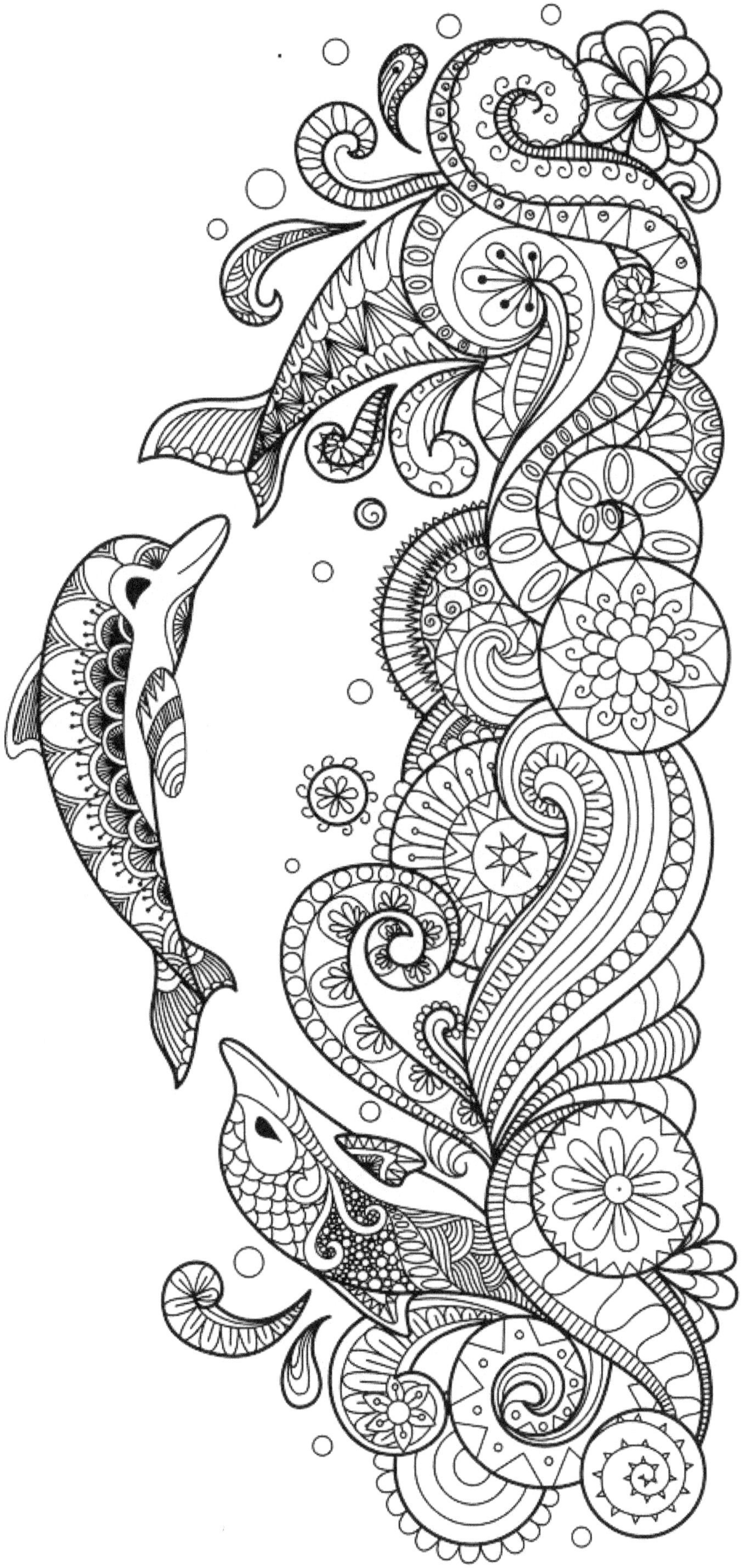

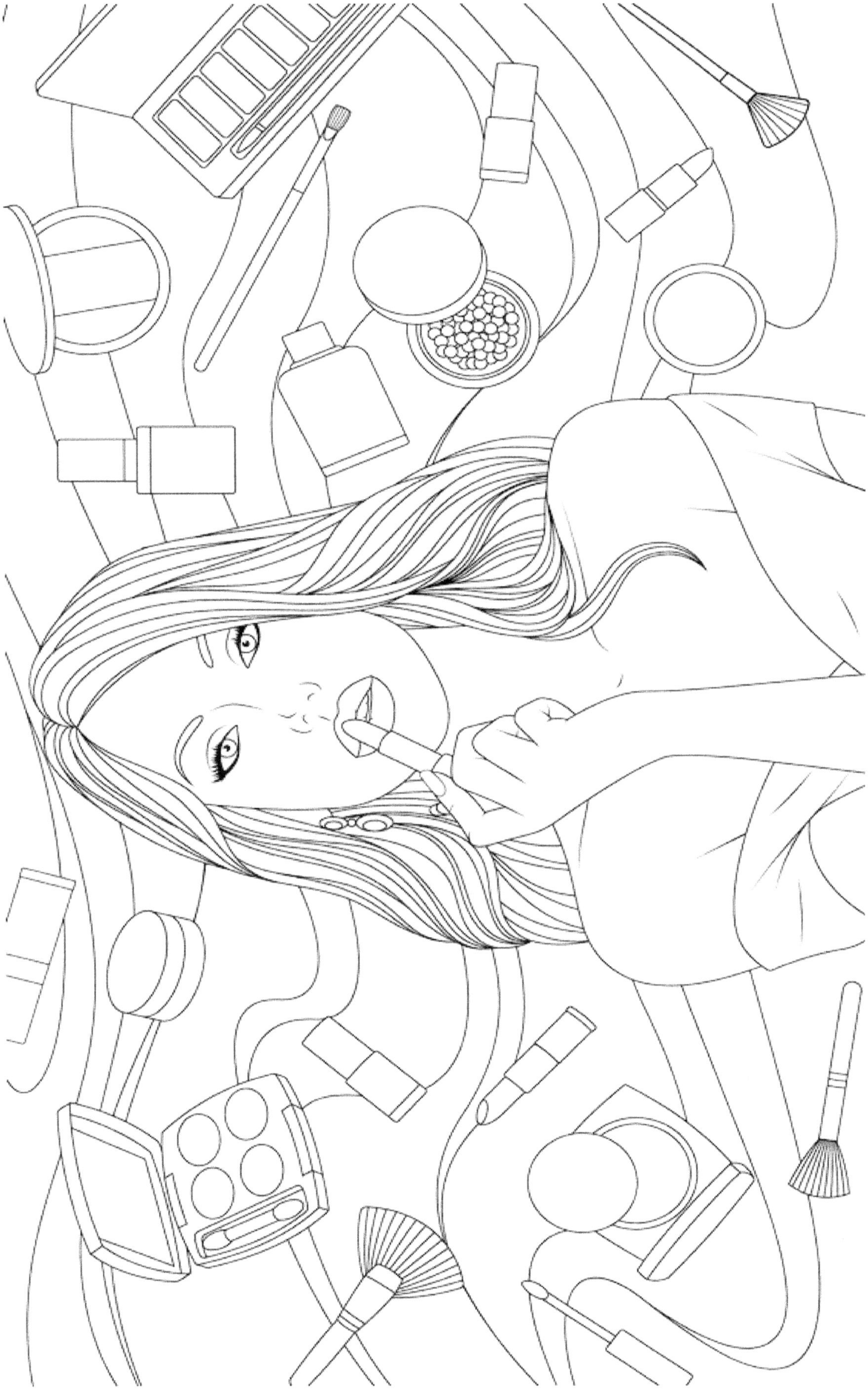

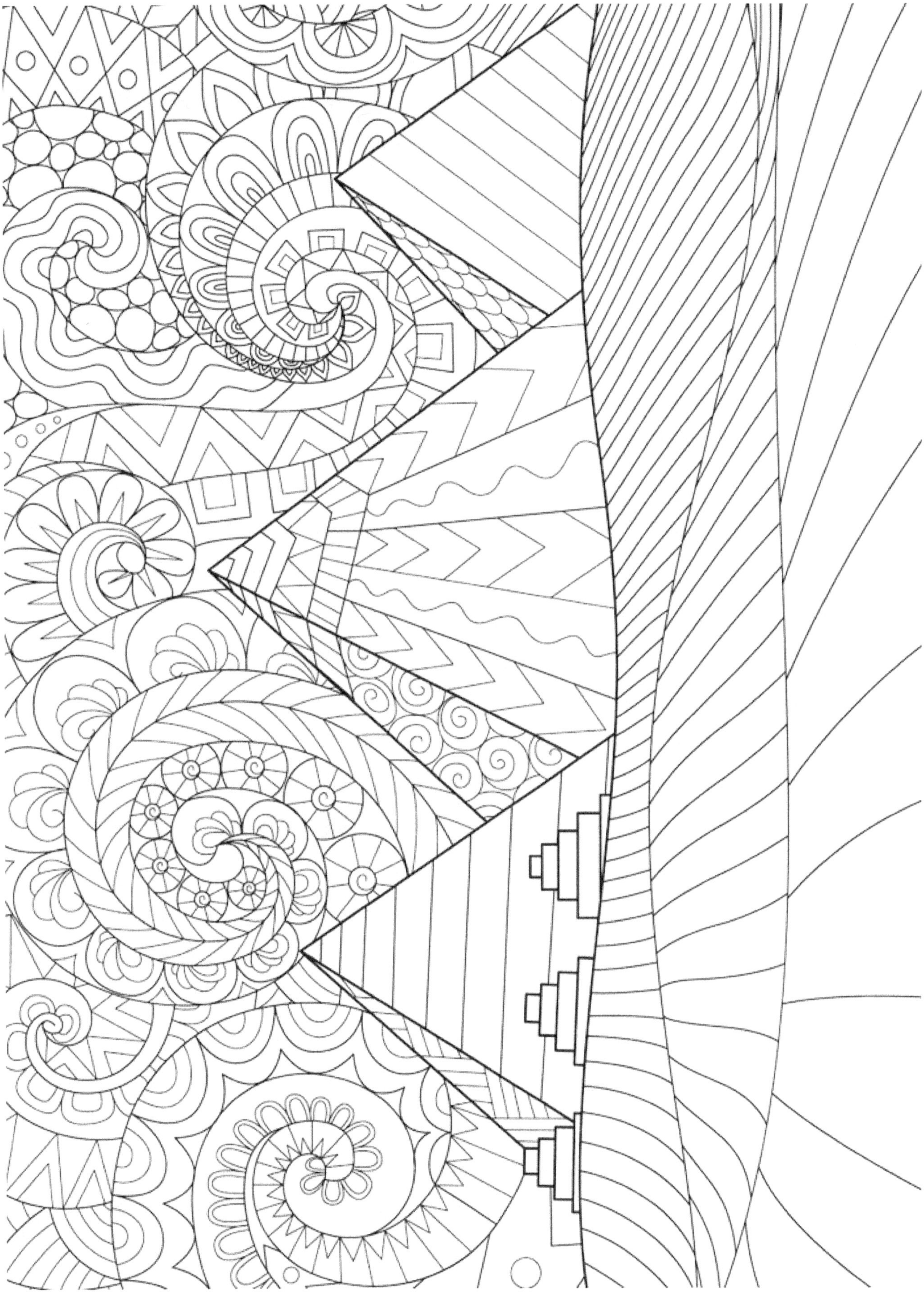

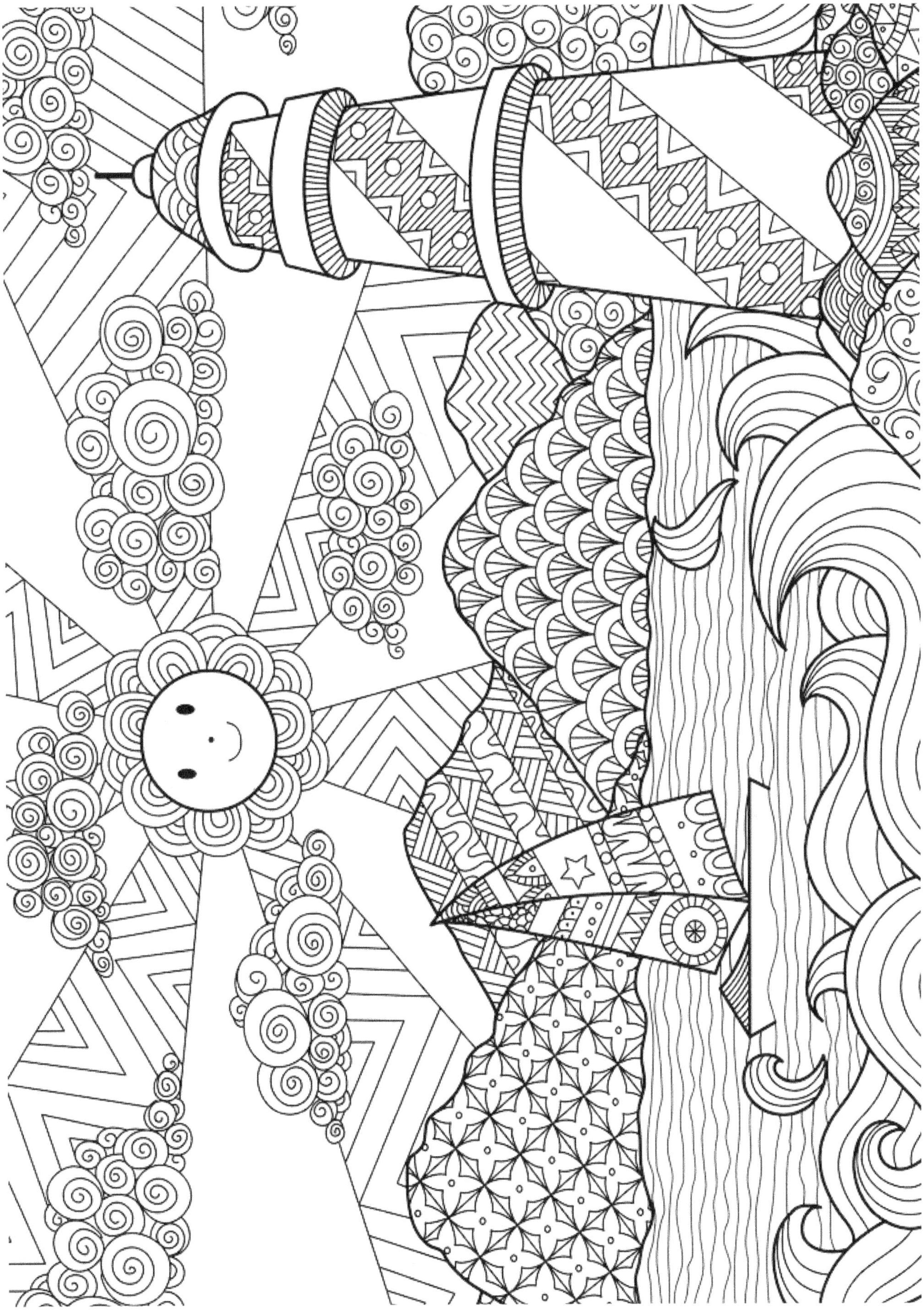

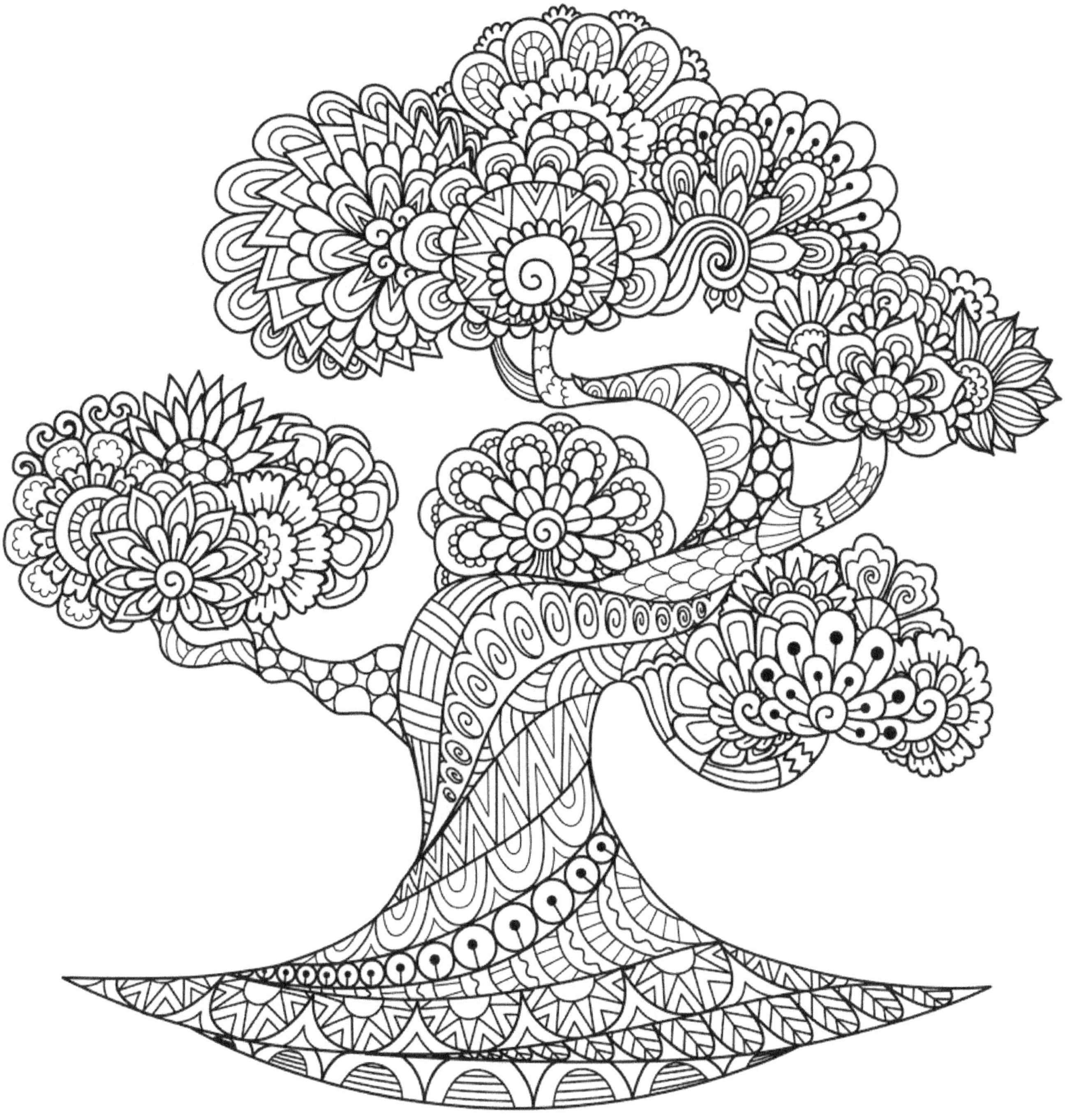

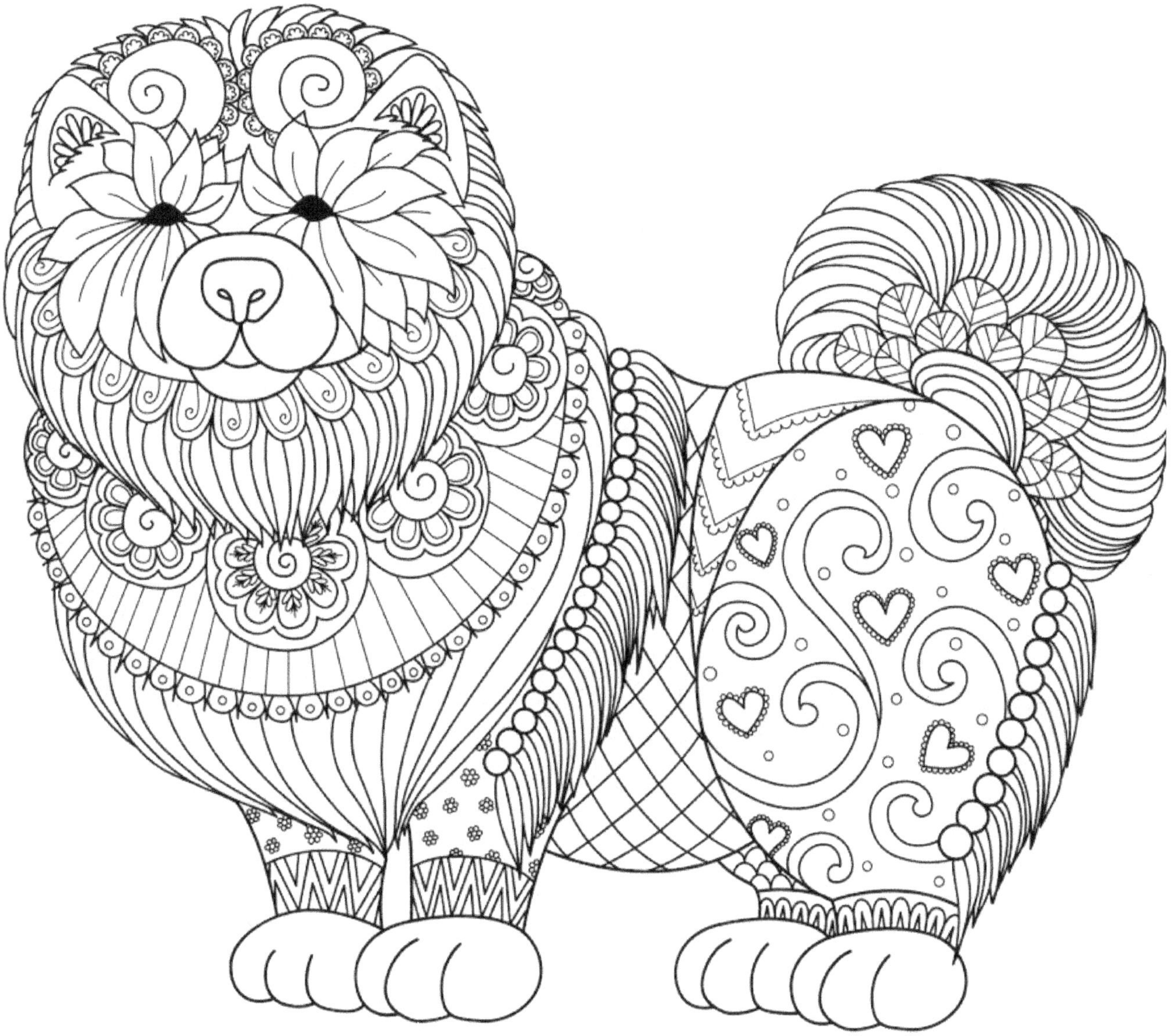

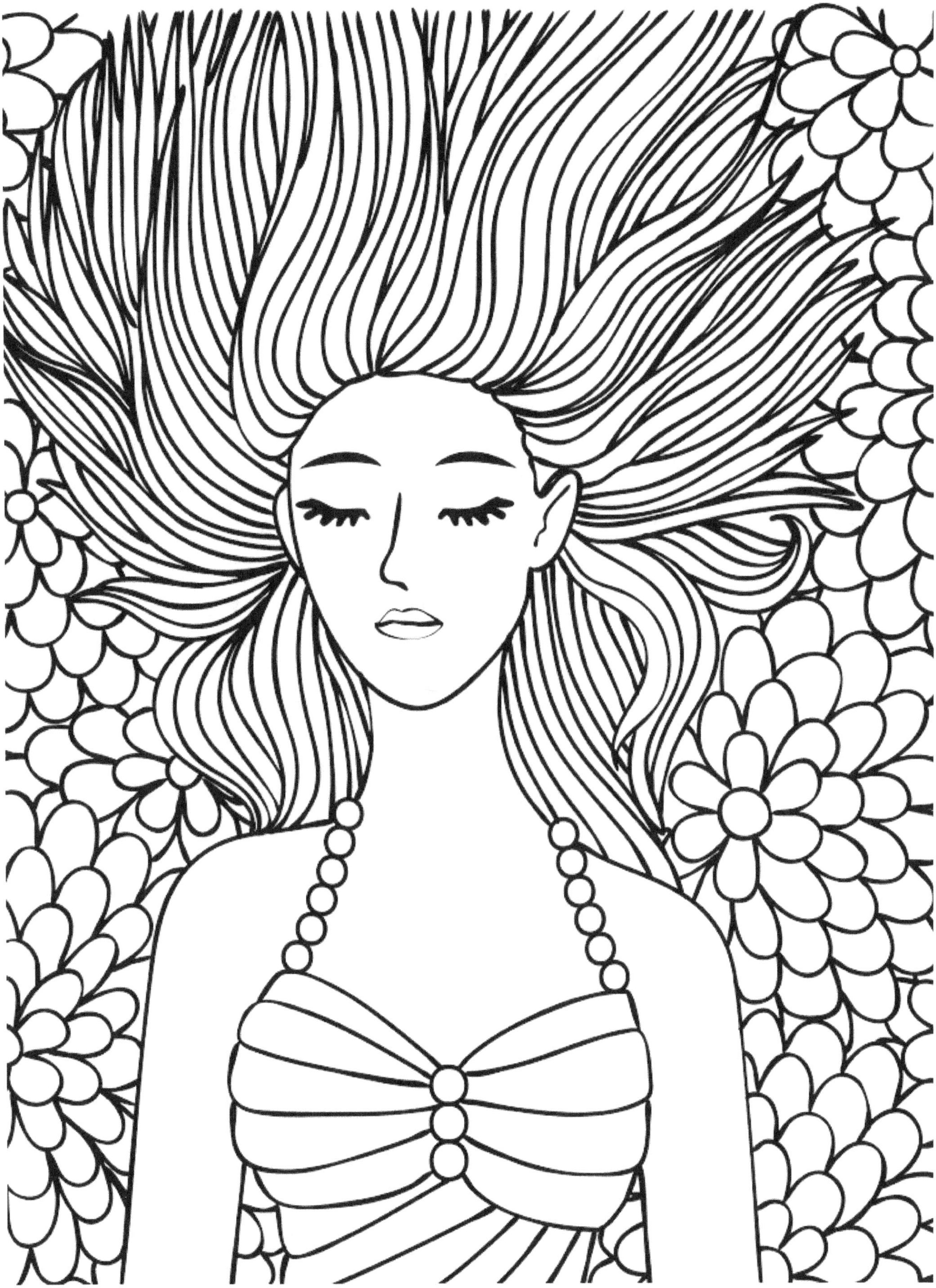

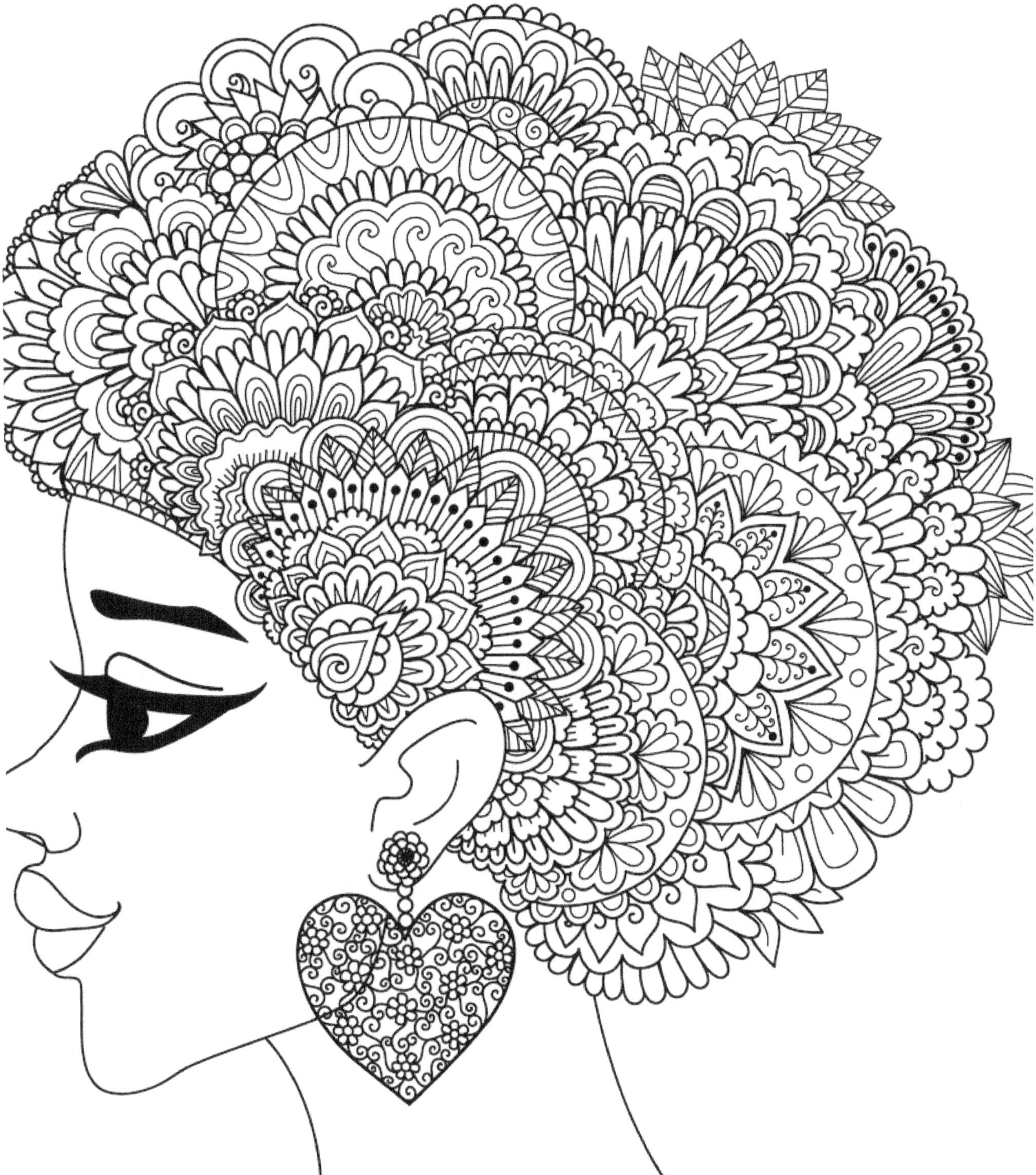

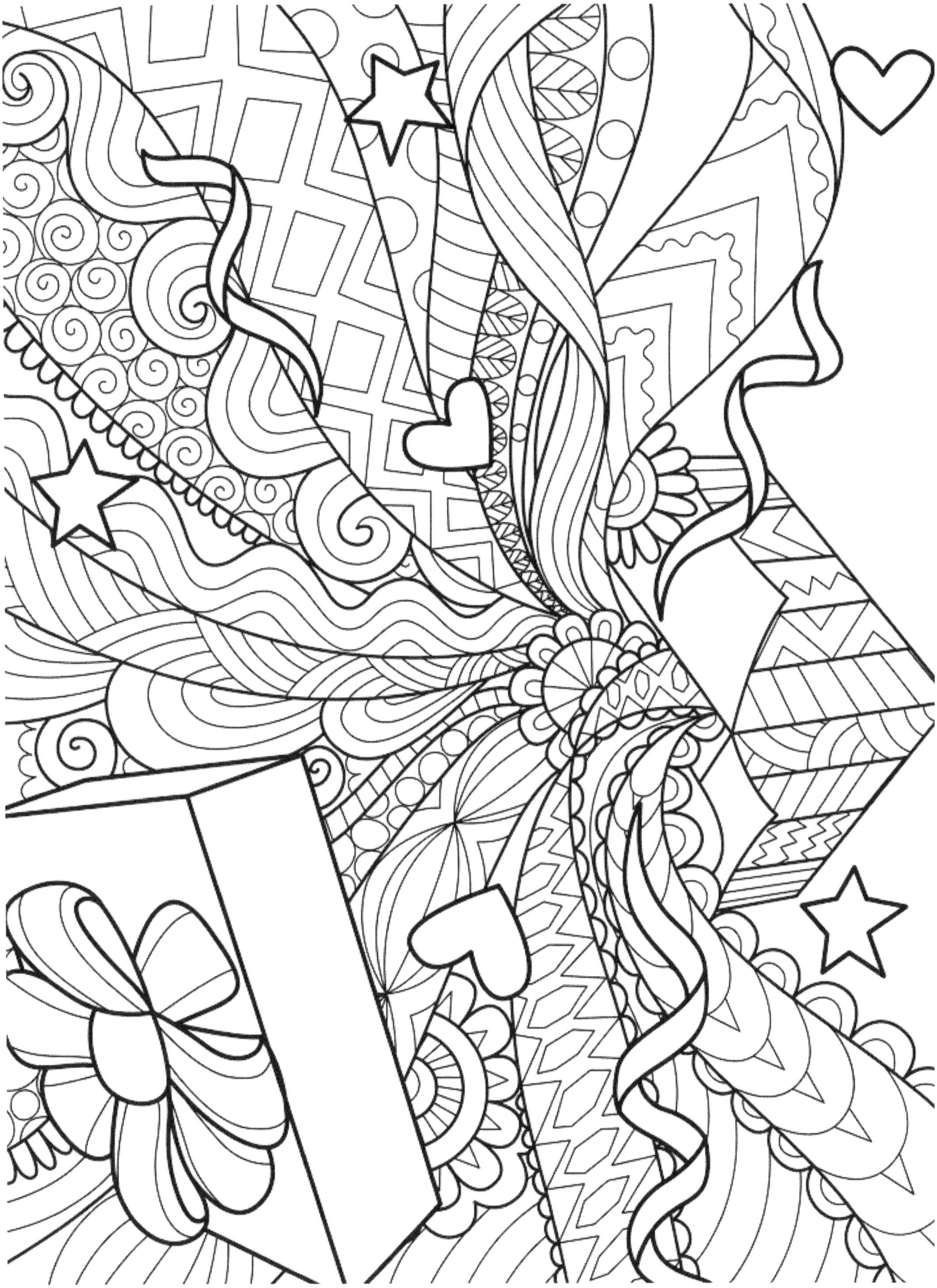

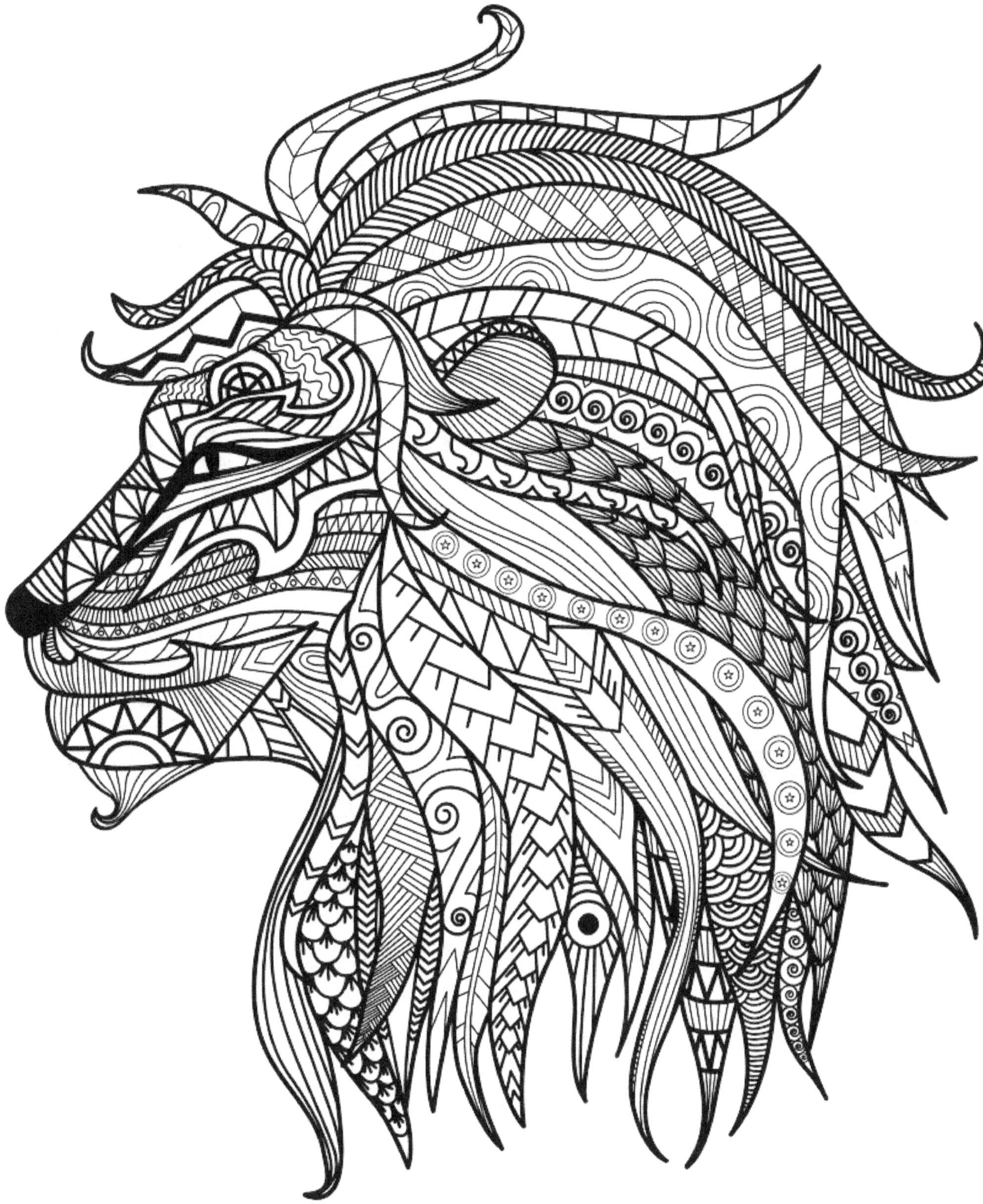

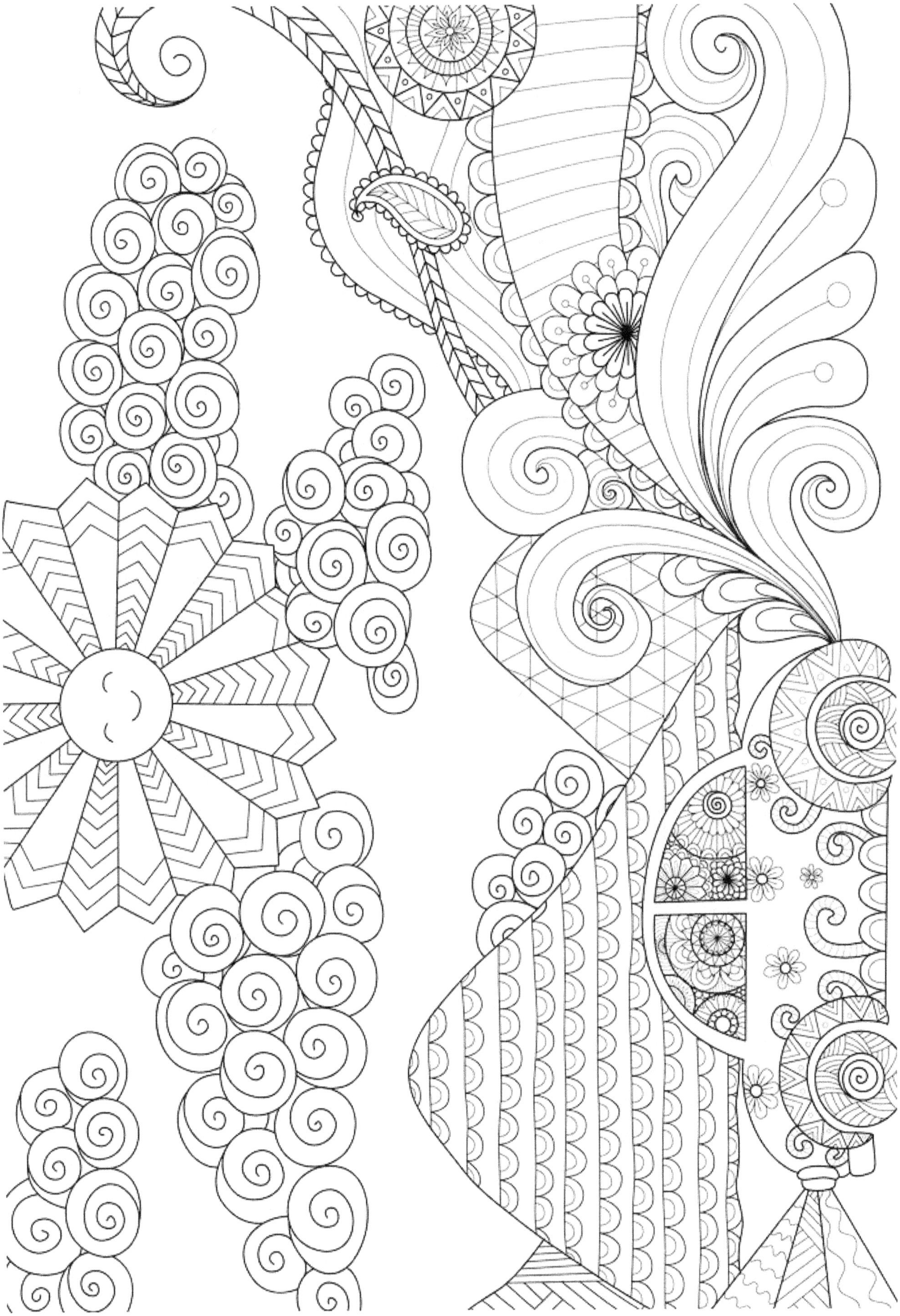

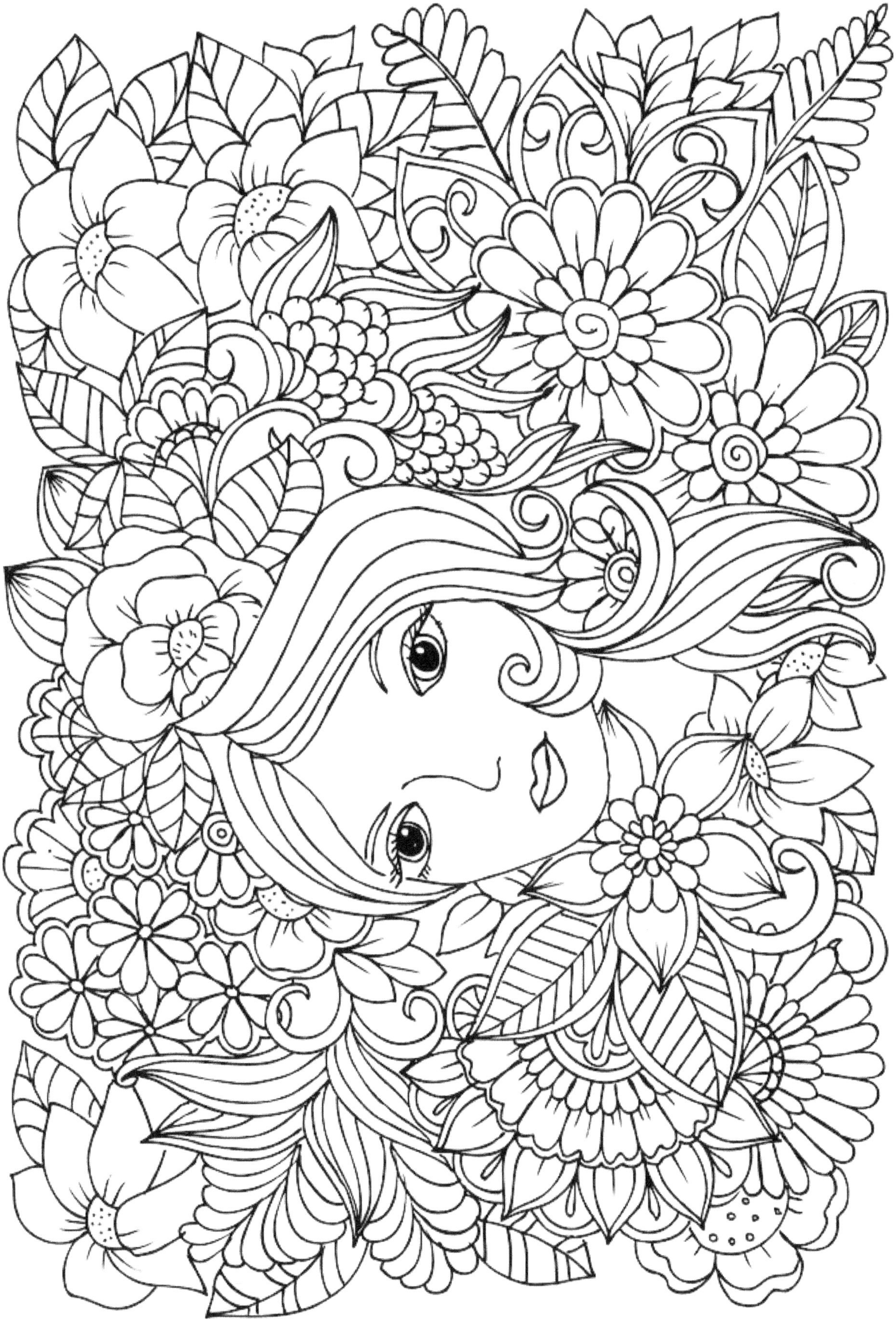

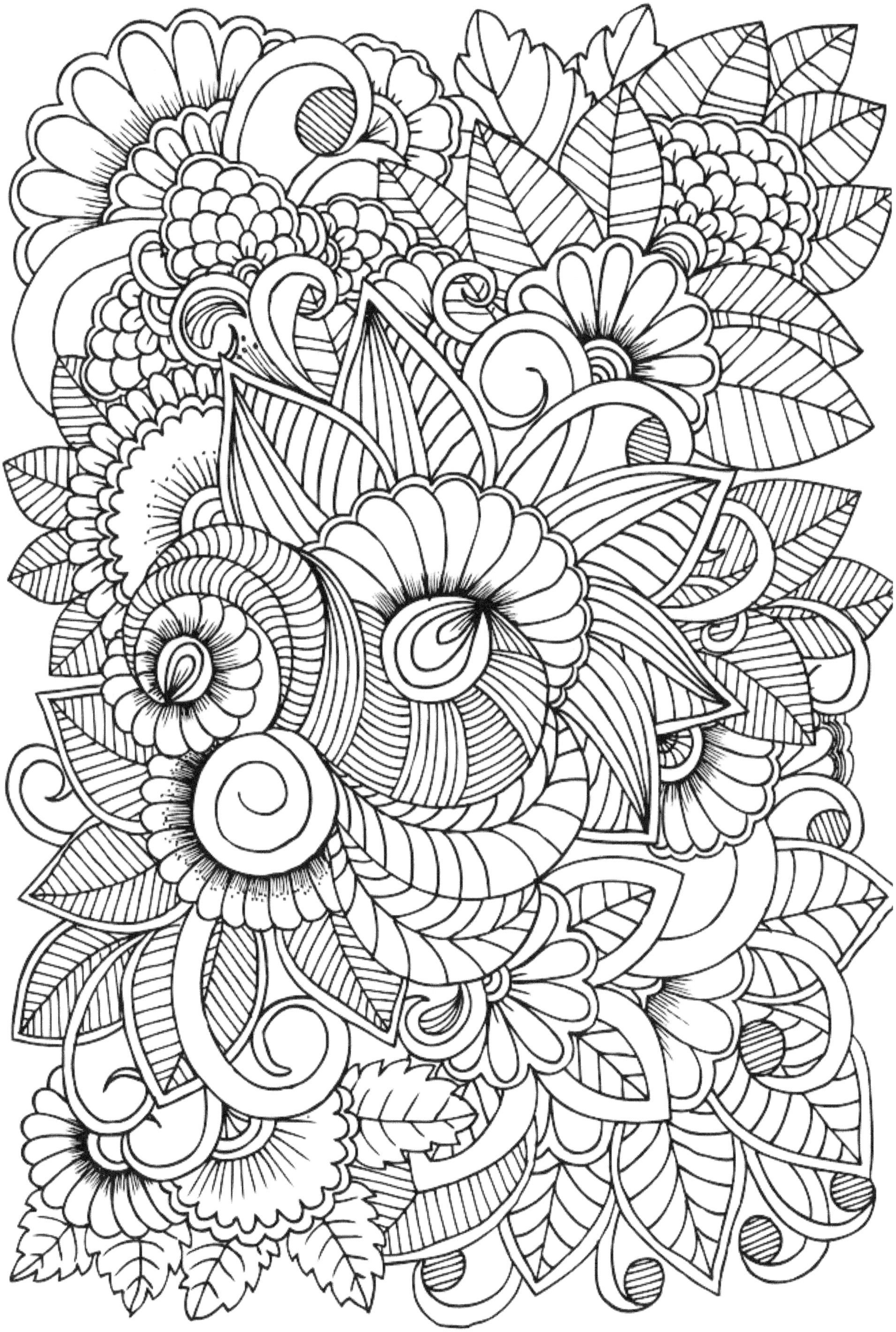

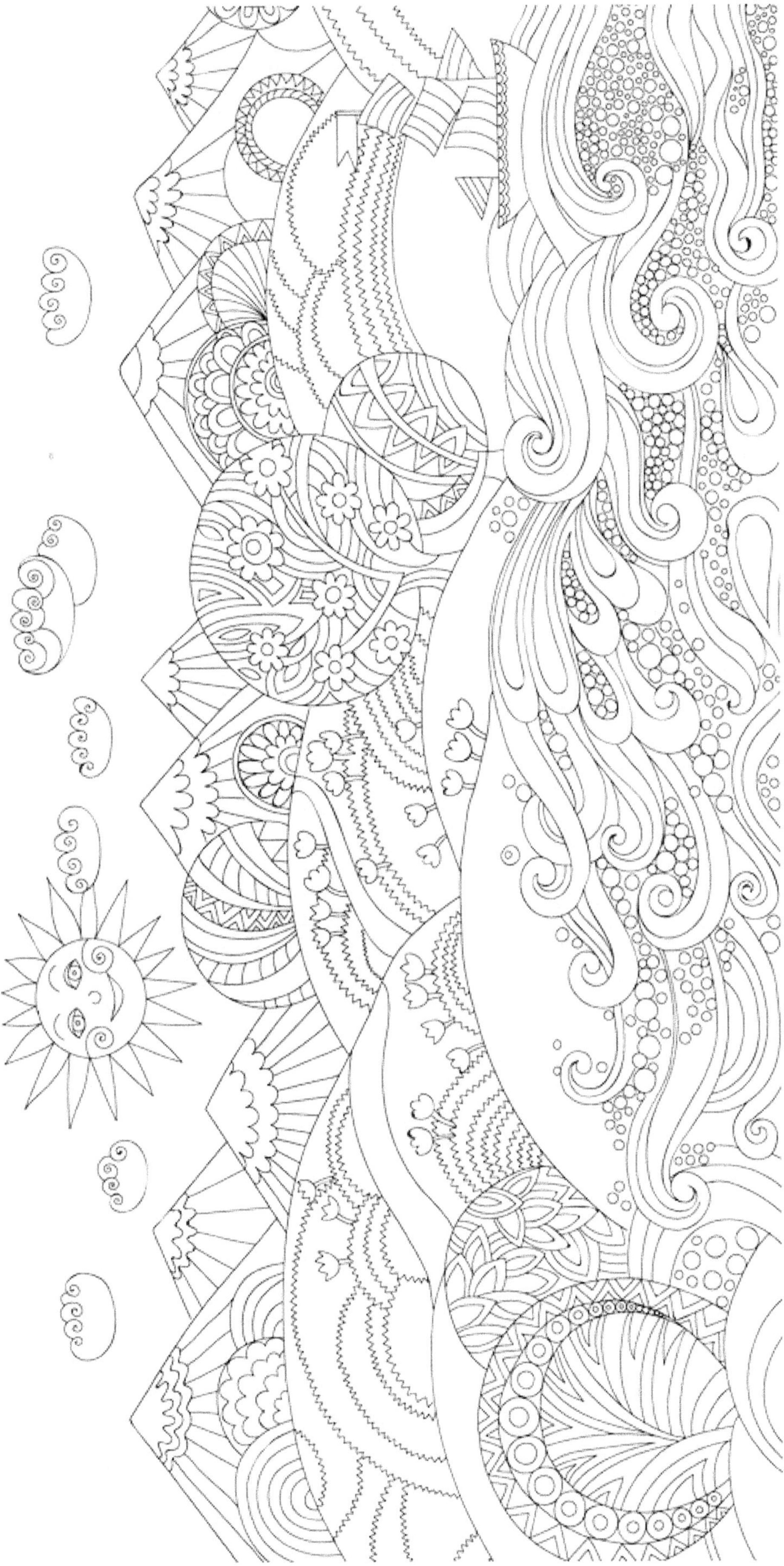

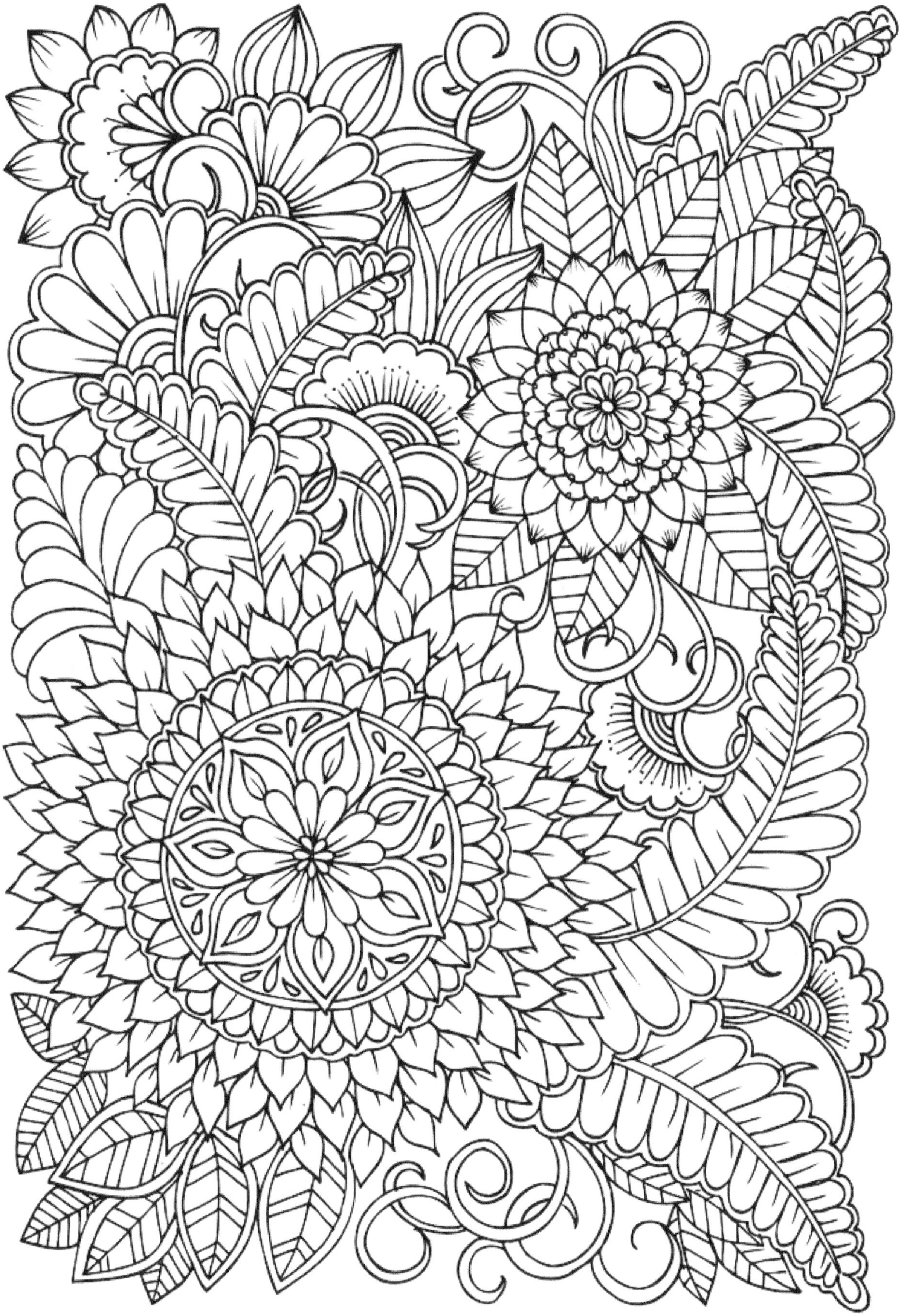

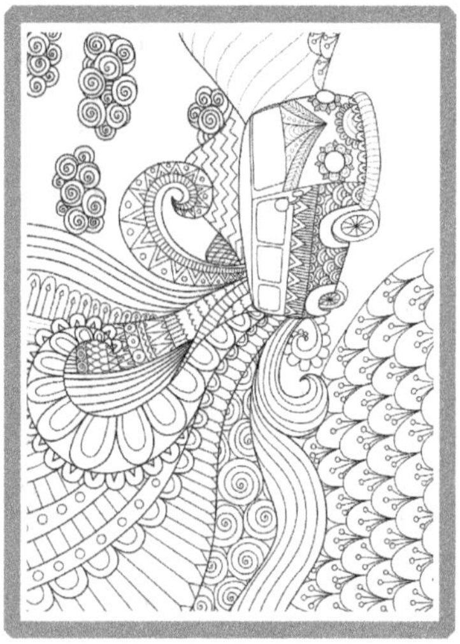
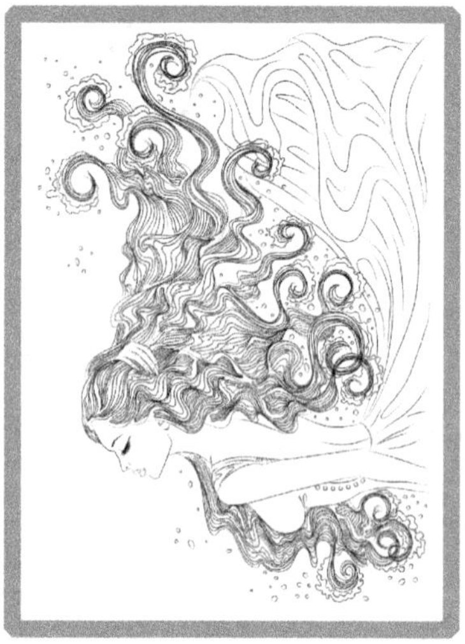
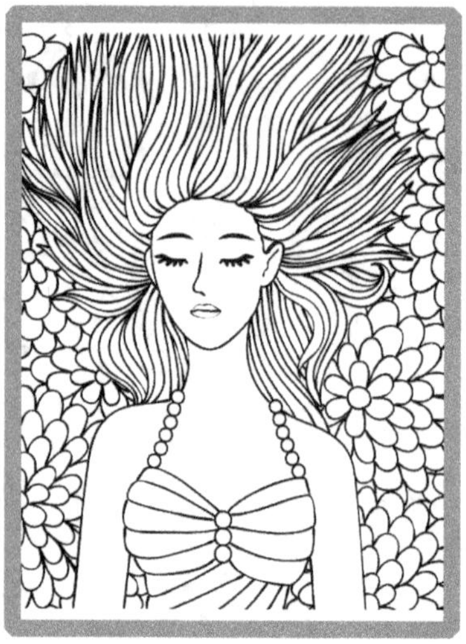
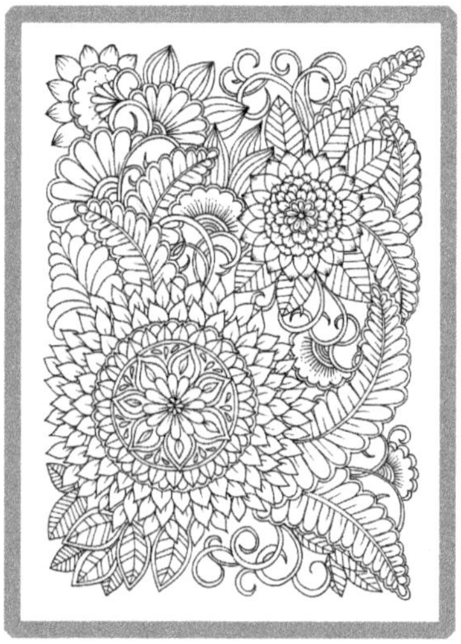
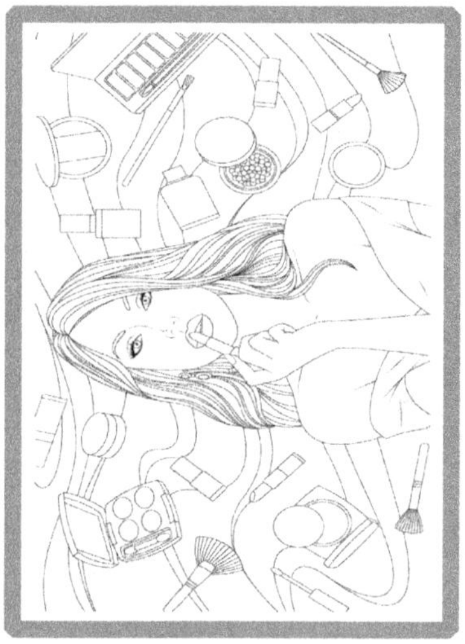
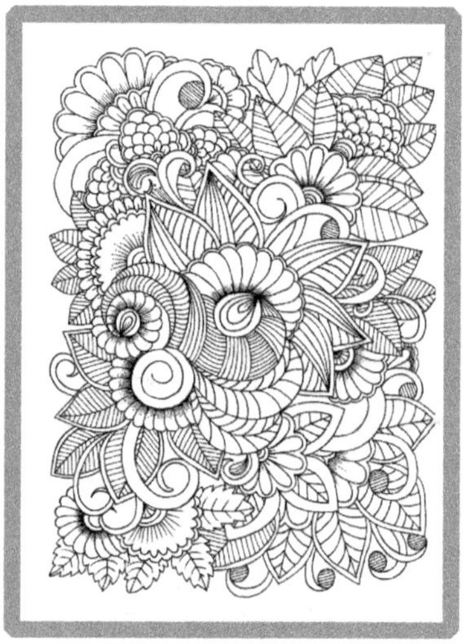
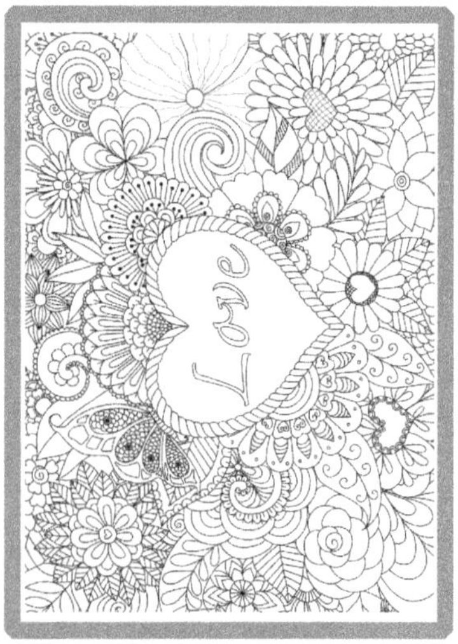
Love
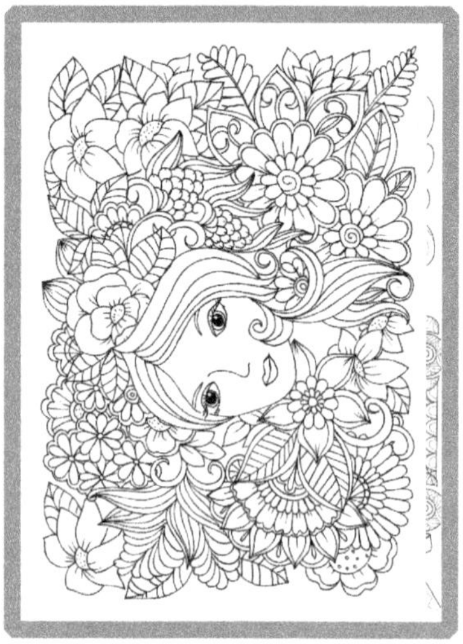
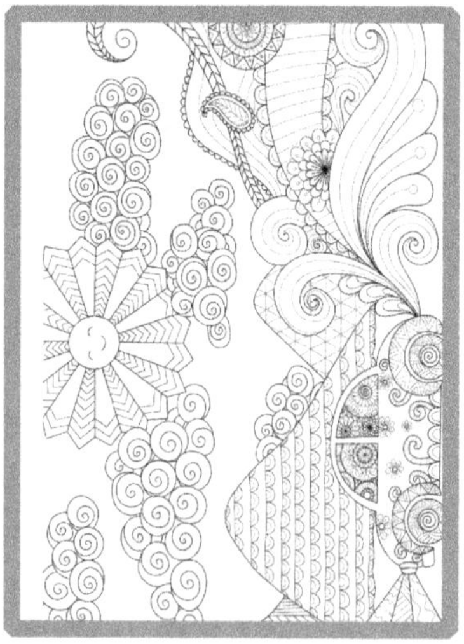

www.ingramcontent.com/pod-product-compliance
Lightning Source LLC
Chambersburg PA
CBHW082148230526
45467CB00043B/2409
* 9 7 9 8 7 0 4 8 4 9 2 5 4 *